Essential
Sides & Sauces

Naturally gluten, dairy, and soy-free
recipes to please every palate

BY ABBY FAMMARTINO OF ABBY'S TABLE

abby's table

Copyright © 2014 by Abby Fammartino
All rights reserved
Cover design by Sika Stanton
Visit the author's website at www.abbys-table.com

FIRST EDITION

DESIGN BY

Jen Wick Studio
jenwickstudio.com

Polara Studio
polarastudio.com

COOKBOOK PHOTOS BY

SikaPhotography
sikaphotography.com

david lanthan reamer
photography
DLReamer.com

SPECIAL THANKS TO

My designer, Jen Wick, for getting this cookbook done with speed and style; my editor, Lois Swagerty, for her amazing thoroughness and attention to detail; my assistant and chief recipe tester, Mia Tarte, for lots of help and enthusiasm in the process; my friend and photographer, Sika Stanton, for doing the cover and taking countless photos for me over the years; my mom, Toni Fammartino, and friend, Michelle Martinez for expert recipe testing and overall support for my work; my husband, Eric, for being the best recipe eater around, in addition to being my biggest support and love in life; my family for years of testing and eating my recipes, and providing genuine encouragement when I needed it the most; and my friends for always being there for me, especially when I have just made a lot of food.

TABLE OF CONTENTS

CHEF'S INTRO

TAKE A BEAUTIFUL, WELL-GROWN, RIPE vegetable. Prepare it well to accentuate the natural properties and flavor. Then top it off with a brilliant, bold, and colorful sauce.

This is the magic of the kitchen. Vegetables, whether raw, panfried to a crisp in coconut oil, or perfectly roasted, are an essential part of life. However, not everyone lines up at the kitchen table for plain-Jane greens and unseasoned tubers. To make healthful ingredients work to support a vibrant lifestyle, it's important to dress them up just right.

I've chosen to focus this cookbook on what I truly think are the most important types of recipes to have in your kitchen "toolbox." Meals come together in a pinch when you have on hand a couple of tasty toppings or dipping sauces that suddenly pull everything together into a cohesive meal. Roasted cauliflower shines alongside a slightly spicy romesco sauce; squash and sage, happy bedfellows, take a quick bath in hot coconut oil, then pair with the vegan lemon aioli to make for a pleasurable eating moment.

It's hard to eat saucy vegetables or main dishes standing up or driving in your car. I love them for this reason, among many others. The recipes in this cookbook should call you to the table, where you can sit and relish the work you've done to create something sublime. Enjoy each bite, and everything will taste better.

Cooking itself is indeed transcendent. You take disparate elements such as vegetables, oils, citrus, nuts and add fire (or simply the fast motion of a blender), and suddenly you have something more than the ingredients themselves. Not only is cooking something pleasurable to do in your spare time, it's something that's essential to life itself.

We need to eat every day, multiple times a day. And though we continue to have more access to ready-to-go, prepared foods that leave our kitchens clean and our ovens cold, it also becomes increasingly difficult to eat for health when relying on packaged and restaurant foods alone. All my recipes are naturally free of gluten, dairy, and soy (three of the most common food allergens) so that you can cook for every type of eater and enjoy good health through fresh foods.

This book is my first of what I hope will be many. It's my mission as a chef to share my recipes with you, your friends, your family, and coworkers, in the hopes that we together can ignite a new (yet very old) food movement that brings people back into the kitchen, and most importantly, back around the table celebrating and enjoying the small moments of life. The culture around our food can be so rich and, as with many things, best enjoyed in the comfort of your home with the ones you love most.

Like a great sauce, food brings people together. I hope you share these recipes with others and invite yourself to the magical world of cooking these essential recipes.

Chef Abby, at work in the kitchen.

COOKING FROM SCRATCH

ALL THE FOOD WE EAT STARTS WITH ingredients that come together to form something more than the sum of its parts.

A seed, good dirt, sunshine, and water yield a perfectly sweet carrot. A perfectly sweet carrot, olive oil, salt, and a flame yield a simple and satisfying sautéed side dish. If it's not you, someone is responsible for the careful growth and preparation of all we consume.

We have a choice: to be the conductor of mealtime or to allow someone else to do it. In a best-case scenario, you are in control of the food you eat—not to an extreme, but to a healthy degree. When you cook from scratch and know how to feed yourself, you have the power to create just what you crave. You have the control over what you buy, how you prepare it, and what the end result tastes like. You know what oils you use (and why) and spend a bit more time with your produce than when it's ready-to-go and chopped for you in a salad.

Most importantly, you have the chance to gain a greater sense of satisfaction from the food itself because of the time and energy spent making it into something nourishing and delicious.

My dream in life is to inspire people to carve out more time for the kitchen so that they can enjoy cooking more and spend more time with loved ones around the table, in community and celebration. Since we all need to eat, knowing how to cook from scratch is one of the most powerful tools you can have in life—for health, for necessity, and for the enjoyment of life itself.

Cook well, eat well. I hope you find a kernel of inspiration somewhere in this book that incites you to make something delightful, and that you find it rewarding. It might just be the little things in life that make the biggest changes.

Clockwise from top left: Coconut Sweet Cream tops a dessert, a young cooking class participant at work, sautéed bok choy prepared for a dinner party, and a happy class participant whipping up dessert.

ESSENTIAL SIDES & SAUCES

PART 1

Fritters and Sides

AS A YOUNG GIRL I NEVER ONCE DREAMT ABOUT fritters. They're not the stuff of fairy tales, yet they are somehow a magical thing. Take a mushy mix of grated vegetables, flour, and oil, and with patience and the right method you create a thin, crispy, savory treat that flies off the table before all other foods.

Of course, this cookbook includes more than just the art of the fritter, but I do think this is one of the most important things I can share with you: how to perfectly crisp panfried bits of vegetable, grains, beans, or a combination of the three.

Why learn about fritters? Because everyone enjoys a good "something fried" once in a while. Need we discuss french fries? I think not. Among all ages and cultures, "crispy fried" is a texture we crave, and a perfect complement to a myriad of dipping sauces and condiments—the aromatic, spicy, bold, and the creamy. Each type of sauce has its place alongside a plate of hot fritters.

There are so many ways to please.

Fritters also seem like a food you shouldn't eat every day, one that requires a huge amount of unhealthful hot oil, and the labors of standing over a wildly hot stove sweating to make a few morsels of crispy deliciousness. This is indeed one way to do it.

But, there are many ways to fry a fritter. With my recipes and panfrying technique, the overbearing heat and large tub of oil will not be your plight.

For less complex vegetable combinations, I've included a section on simple, delicious preparations with vegetables. Please use your imagination and substitute different veggies using the techniques in my recipes. I encourage innovation and utilizing what you have on hand. Master the techniques over time, and you will soon have more reasons than not to buy beautiful vegetables.

How to Fry a Fritter

Start by heating a skillet over medium heat.
Add a thin layer of oil, just enough to coat the bottom of the pan.

Here's the long and short of becoming the mayor of Fritterville, in four easy steps.

1. Scoop and flatten. Use a regular spoon or a small ice cream scoop to scoop out the batter directly into the pan. Leave room around each fritter and work in a clockwise fashion so you know which ones to flip first. Use the back of the spoon to flatten the batter into a circle in the pan, so you have a fritter shape.

2. Wait for the brown edges. This is the part that requires patience. Don't flip even one fritter too soon—the batter will stick to your spatula and ruin the shape of the fritter, as well as dirty the oil with fritter bits and pieces. Just wait until you see browning happening around the edge of the fritters. This takes about 2 minutes, though it will be more for the very first batch (just like pancakes).

3. Flip the furthest from you. Once the edges are brown it's time to flip. Using a towel or hot pad, hold the handle of the pan and move it so that the fritter you are flipping is always at 12 o'clock (the furthest away from you). Once you flip, flatten the browned side with the back of your spatula. Move the handle in whatever direction you need so that the next fritter you fry is still in the 12-o'clock position. Continue with each fritter in the pan.

4. Be mindful of your heat. You are now on the second side —the easy part! Wait another 2 minutes or so until the second side is nicely browned before removing the fritters from the pan and onto a towel-lined plate or tray. Do not let your oil get too hot at this point. Monitor the oil so it is always at about medium heat. This will be different for everyone, depending on your heat source (electric, gas, or induction stovetop). Mind the medium, and you will be sure not to overheat the oil.

TOOLS

Here are the things you'll need to succeed for a lifetime of flipping fritters in your kitchen.

A METAL SPATULA—a sturdy metal spatula is best for cleanly flipping fritters.

A GOOD QUALITY, MEDIUM-SIZE SKILLET—you don't want a skillet that is too large, as it will be hard to conduct even heat across the pan to crisp up each fritter. I love my 10-inch all-clad pan and 12-inch cast-iron pan for fritters.

A HOT PAD OR TOWEL—for holding the handle of the skillet as you flip.

A DOUGH SCRAPER (or scraper tool) —for scraping crispy bits off the metal spatula as you go; a clean spatula is key.

THE RIGHT OIL FOR THE JOB—I love coconut oil for medium-high heat frying, as it's an easily digestible oil that is high in healthy cholesterol and is anti-inflammatory. My second choice might surprise you: it's well-sourced animal lard. It is suitable for medium-high heat oil and has been made for generations with little refining and fussing. Avocado oil, grapeseed oil, and safflower oil, though refined oils, are decent substitutes if you really need high heat (also see glossary).

TOWELS TO ABSORB EXCESS OIL

Expert level:
A METAL OR GLASS BOWL WITH A STRAINER SET OVER TOP—This is for cleaning the brown bits out of your pan as you continue frying, so that you can refresh the oil and safely discard the used hot oil.

CHAPTER 1
Fritters

NOW THAT YOU'VE LEARNED THE TECHNIQUE, try it with the following fritter recipes. I hope you will be confident navigating other panfried recipes using this technique as well. The six recipes I share with you are recipes that can be made with many variations, so please use your own creative whims to make these your own.

Substitute different grains for quinoa in the quinoa sweet potato cakes, different root vegetables with the season in the crispy root vegetable fritters, and cannellini or adzuki beans for the chickpeas in the chickpea and herb fritters. Pick your fancy!

Let's get frying.

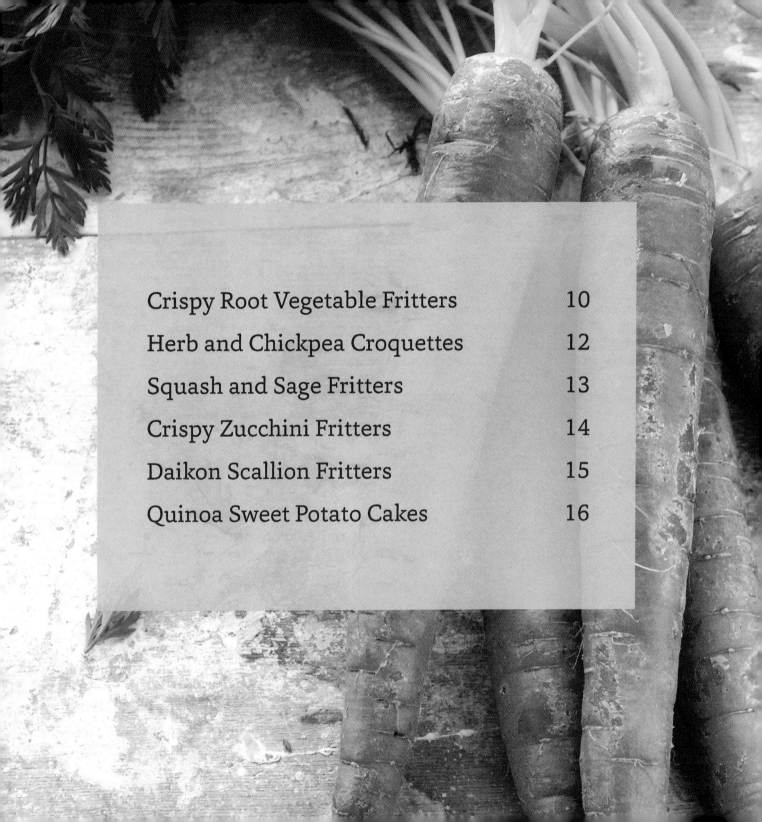

Crispy Root Vegetable Fritters

Serves: 6–8 (20 fritters)

This is one of my most popular recipes. It's versatile and easy to prepare as long as you follow the cooking instructions to a tee. Don't be in too much of a hurry when making these or you are likely to flip too soon, yielding mushy fritters and a messy pan, or leave them in too long, yielding burnt fritters that won't taste like anything! Patience and focus are the secret ingredients.

1 lb. root vegetable of choice (about 2 large beets, 1 celery root, 6 parsnips or carrots)
¾ tsp. sea salt
⅔ cup olive oil
½ cup gluten-free all-purpose flour

½–⅔ cup coconut oil, for frying

1. Wash the vegetables well. Remove ends (and, for celery root only, peel the vegetable following its shape.) Grate manually, or use the matchstick blade on a food processor, if available to you. You should end up with about 4 1/2–5 cups grated vegetables.

2. Add sea salt to the olive oil, stirring to dissolve. Add the salted oil and flour to grated vegetables, and mix well with hands. Batter should be wet enough for you to form little balls easily.

3. Place bowl of batter near the frying pan and grab a tablespoon. Heat a thin layer of coconut oil to start, over medium heat. Oil should coat the bottom of the pan evenly.

4. Once oil is hot, spoon a rounded tablespoon of batter into the pan and form each fritter into a circle using the back of the tablespoon to flatten.

5. Do not touch fritters until you notice the bottom edges of the fritters turning brown, about 2 minutes (the first batch will take slightly longer). Flip with a metal spatula, pressing down to flatten the second side of the fritter slightly to ensure that the center cooks nicely. Cook until second side is well browned, another 2 minutes.

6. Remove from hot oil and place on a towel-lined baking sheet or a plate to soak up oil. Keep adding oil as needed to keep a thin layer of oil on the bottom of the pan. You may need to add more oil 2–3 times during the process. Serve immediately.

Try with: Cashew Sour Cream, Horseradish Cream, Lemon Aioli, Garden Ranch Sauce, and any of the pestos.

Crispy Root Vegetable Fritters

Herb and Chickpea Croquettes

Serves: 6–8 (20 fritters)

Here is a fritter that can function as a main dish in a vegetarian meal. Combining legumes and whole grains makes for a complete protein, so that you can accompany these power-packed fritters with a simple vegetable and a sauce for any meal, super casual or super fancy!

1 ½ cups cooked chickpeas
1 cup cooked grain (brown rice or quinoa are great)
½ cup shallot or sweet onion, diced
2 garlic cloves, minced
½ cup celery, diced
⅔ cup chopped fresh parsley, chives, dill, or oregano
½ tsp. sea salt, more to taste
1 heaping Tbsp. Dijon mustard
⅓ cup rice cracker bread crumbs (buy plain rice crackers and process until fine)
¼ cup all-purpose gluten-free flour
⅓ cup olive oil

½–⅔ cup coconut oil, for frying

1. Pulse the chickpeas and cooked grain together in food processor, or mash in a bowl with a tool, adding 2 tablespoons olive oil if moisture is needed. Add all remaining ingredients and pulse (or mash in by hand) until evenly blended. Taste for flavor and let sit 10 minutes. If dough seems dry, add more olive oil until you can easily form a ball in your hand. Form into balls no bigger than 2 inches in diameter.

2. Heat a pan with a thin layer of coconut oil over medium heat until hot. Fry croquettes 2 minutes per side, pressing down lightly with a spatula on the second side. Serve immediately or if enjoying later, place on a baking sheet and finish cooking in the oven at 350° F. until browned and crispy on the exterior but not dry, about 5–10 minutes.

3. Replenish oil as needed when frying, changing out oil if brown bits form (scrape oil into a bowl lined with a strainer so you can use the oil once more for panfrying).

Try with: Any of the pestos, Raw Tomato Sauce, Romesco Sauce, Lemon Aioli, or Cashew Sour Cream.

Squash and Sage Fritters

Serves: 6–8 (20 fritters)

No grating is necessary for this fritter recipe. Instead the squash or pumpkin is cooked and mashed. This is a lovely fall recipe and, of course, feel free to experiment with different root vegetables in winter, such as parsnips or celery root. Switch up the fresh herb to rosemary and you have a whole new fritter recipe to include as a side to your meal!

2 ½ cups pumpkin or winter squash (about one squash)
½ tsp. sea salt, plus more to taste
⅔ cup olive oil
½ cup gluten-free all-purpose flour (or brown rice flour)
3 Tbsp. chopped sage

½–⅔ cup coconut oil, for frying

1. Cook the pumpkin or squash: Peel, deseed and dice pumpkin/squash and cover with water. Bring to a boil and cook until soft, about 10 minutes. Strain and mash in a bowl.

2. Add sea salt to the olive oil, stirring to dissolve. Add the salted oil and flour to cooked squash and mix well with hands. Add in chopped sage. Batter should be soft; you will be spooning batter into the pan. Place batter near stove and set out a baking sheet for the finished fritters, as you will work in batches.

3. Heat a thin layer of coconut oil to start, over medium heat. Oil should evenly coat the bottom of the pan.

4. Once oil is hot, place several fritters in the pan. Use a tablespoon to drop batter into the pan, and use the back of the spoon to spread the batter into a small circle.

5. Do not touch fritters until you notice the bottom edges of the fritters turning brown, about 2 minutes (the first batch will take slightly longer). Flip with a metal spatula, pressing down to flatten the circle slightly. Cook until second side is well browned, 1–2 minutes more.

6. Remove from hot oil and place on a baking sheet or a plate with a paper towel to soak up oil. Keep adding oil as needed to keep a thin layer of oil on the bottom of the pan. You may need to add more oil 2–3 times during the process. Serve immediately.

Try with: Simple Cider Sauce, Rosemary Hazelnut Pesto, Fennel Yogurt Sauce, Horseradish Cream, Garden Ranch Sauce.

Crispy Zucchini Fritters

Serves 6–8 (16–20 fritters)

Here's a lovely summertime and fall fritter using zucchini or summer squash. This recipe is similar to the root vegetable fritters; however, it's important to add the salt to the zucchini first to squeeze out excess water. This way your oil won't splash back at you when you add the batter to the hot pan. A nice bonus!

1 lb. summer squash (about 3 medium zucchini)
½ tsp. sea salt, plus more to taste
⅔ cup extra virgin olive oil
½ cup gluten-free all-purpose flour

½ cups coconut oil, for frying

1. Wash the zucchini/summer squash and remove ends. Grate manually, or use the matchstick blade on a food processor, if available to you. You should end up with 4 1/2–5 cups grated vegetable. Add the sea salt to the zucchini in a strainer placed over a bowl. Let the vegetables sit for 5–10 minutes to expel excess water. Strain over a sink, squeezing the salted squash in your hands to release the water.

2. Add extra virgin olive oil to the salted squash in a bowl. Add the flour and mix well with hands. Batter should be wet; you will be spooning batter into the pan. Place batter near stove and set out a baking sheet for the finished fritters, as you will work in batches.

3. Heat a thin layer of coconut oil to start, over medium heat. Oil should evenly coat the bottom of the pan.

4. Once oil is hot, place several fritters in the pan. Use a tablespoon to drop batter into the pan, and use the back of the spoon to spread the batter into a small circle.

5. Do not touch fritters until you notice the bottom edges of the fritters turning brown, about 2 minutes (the first batch will take slightly longer). Flip with a metal spatula, pressing down to flatten the circle slightly. Cook until second side is well browned, 2 minutes more.

6. Remove from hot oil and place on a baking sheet or a plate with a paper towel to soak up some oil. Keep adding oil as needed to keep a thin layer of oil on the bottom of the pan. You may need to add more oil 2–3 times during the process. Serve immediately.

Try with: Raw Tomato Sauce, Romesco Sauce, Fennel Yogurt Sauce, Charmoula.

Daikon Scallion Fritters

Serves: 6–8 (20 fritters)

These fritters are fairly addictive. The batter holds well for a couple days, so you can easily panfry a few as a side dish to a simple salad meal whenever you desire something crispy and hot. Daikon is in the radish family, and is a great aid to the body in digesting fats and fried foods. Use an egg replacer to make these vegan, if needed.

2 cups gluten free all-purpose flour
1 egg, beaten
1 ½ cups water
⅓ cup olive oil
1 large bunch scallions, sliced thinly into rings (top and bottom)
3 cups shredded daikon radish
1 ¼ tsp. salt (plus more to taste)

½ cup coconut oil, for frying

1. Mix all ingredients together and let sit for about 10 minutes or more (great do-ahead recipe!).
2. Stir well before cooking to ensure flour doesn't settle to the bottom. Check consistency before cooking; batter should be a little runny like American pancake batter, so that the cakes cook quickly and evenly.
3. Heat a sauté pan over medium heat until hot, then add a thin layer of coconut oil.
4. Spoon batter into the pan using a tablespoon and smooth out the daikon into an even circle. I like to move the bowl with me so I don't drip the batter everywhere on the way to the place I'm dropping it in the pan.
5. Cook for 2 minutes until bubbling throughout, and golden brown on bottom.
6. Flip and finish by cooking 2 more minutes. Add more oil to the pan as you go to keep a thin layer going as you cook off the whole batch (or the amount you plan to cook).
7. Garnish with coarse salt or serve with a nice sauce.

Try with: Fennel Yogurt Sauce, Spicy Plum Chutney, Tamarind Glaze, Almond Peanut Sauce (use sesame oil in the recipe in place of olive oil!), Garden Ranch Sauce, Garlic Aioli.

Quinoa Sweet Potato Cakes

Serves 8: 32 cakes (freezes well)

These cakes are very versatile and a great grain side dish to pull together a meal that has a saucy entreé such as a ragout, a braised dish, or chili. They serve as a great complement to a simple meal of a main dish salad as well.

1 ½ cups cooked mashed sweet potato
2 ½ cups cooked quinoa*
1 ½ tsp. sea salt
⅔ cup olive oil
½ cup finely diced onion or shallot
1 cup gluten-free all-purpose flour

½ cup coconut oil, for frying

1. Combine all ingredients and mix well. Coat a frying pan with a thin layer of coconut oil over medium heat.

2. Add cakes (form batter into a tablespoon-size ball) and cook for 2–3 minutes on the first side; do not flip until edges are browned around the side.

3. Use a metal spatula to flip. Cook on the second side for 2 minutes more. Repeat with remaining batter. Rewarm in the oven if making ahead.

Alternatively, grease a cookie sheet with coconut oil and bake in the oven on 425° F., flipping the cakes once to brown both sides (about 12 minutes total).

*To cook the quinoa: measure 1 1/2 cups quinoa and 3 cups water in a small pot, with a pinch of salt. Bring to a boil uncovered, and when the water boils, turn down the heat to a simmer and cover the pot. Simmer for 15 minutes, then turn off the heat and allow to steam for 5 minutes more. Now your quinoa is cooked and ready to use!

Try with: Romesco Sauce, Garlic Aioli, Garden Ranch Sauce, Rosemary Hazelnut Pesto, Lavender Berry Chutney.

CHAPTER 2
Assorted Vegetable Sides

WE NEED VEGETABLES EVERY DAY. Sorry if this comes as bad news to you, but we all know it's true. If you are a lover of all things green or ground-grown, maybe you need some new ideas for how to keep things fresh and fun. Vegetables are the key to life—among other important things, such as water, of course.

And since not every vegetable can (or should) be panfried to a crisp, here are some essential techniques with vegetables for everyday meals at home. All of these vegetable sides can be enjoyed plain, or made more flavorful and fancy with a complimentary sauce. With each recipe, I've given some suggestions to mix and match the recipes from this section with those of the subsequent sauce sections, even if it's a sauce suggestion for a main course that accompanies the vegetable dish.

Enjoy! Eat more veggies! Or at least enjoy the veggies you eat more by preparing them well.

Balsamic Asparagus

Serves: 4

This is a very simple oven technique for asparagus. Using high heat and a short cook time, you consistently get simple, flavorful, crisp asparagus. I learned this recipe by watching my mom make it over and over when I was growing up!

2 bunches fresh asparagus, tough lower ends removed
2 Tbsp. balsamic vinegar
1–2 Tbsp. olive oil
½ tsp. sea salt
¼ tsp. fresh pepper, to taste

1. Preheat oven to 425° F. Place asparagus on a baking sheet and drizzle with balsamic vinegar and olive oil. Roll the baking sheet to distribute the liquids evenly, so the asparagus looks well coated.

2. If you have big bunches of asparagus, you may need to use two pans so as to not overcrowd the vegetable. In this case, use your judgement and add more olive oil and balsamic, so the asparagus is well coated.

3. Sprinkle asparagus with salt and pepper. On the top rack of the oven, roast the asparagus until lower ends are bright and crispy, 10–12 minutes only. Roast in two batches if using two trays.

Try with: Garlic Aioli, Lemon Aioli, Spicy Plum Chutney, or Lavender Berry Chutney.

Balsamic Asparagus

Mashed and Roasted Pumpkin

Serves: 4

A fun take on a twice-baked vegetable: boil, mash, and then roast the pumpkin on high heat to make a crispy, creamy side dish.

2 lb. peeled, chopped pumpkin or winter squash (from a 3 lb. pumpkin)
⅓ cup grapeseed or avocado oil
½–¾ tsp. sea salt
¼ tsp. freshly ground black pepper

1. Preheat oven to 425° F.

2. Place chopped pumpkin or squash in a large pot and cover with water, about 2 inches over the vegetables.

3. On high heat, bring to a boil. Boil until pumpkin is fork tender, about 10 minutes.

4. Once squash is fork tender, drain the water out. Generously oil a lined baking sheet (use parchment or a reususable silicon pan liner) and place the pumpkin in an even layer.

5. Use a pint size glass jar or can to smash the pumpkin. Don't overdo it; you want it to hold some shape if possible.

6. Drizzle with oil and season with salt and pepper. Roast for about 25 minutes, flipping once after 15 minutes. You want the pumpkin to get crispy on both sides, and nicely browned.

7. Remove from oven once it is done to your liking, and top with a sprinkle of pepper to finish.

Try with: Raw Tomato Sauce, Romesco Sauce, Fennel Yogurt Sauce, Charmoula.

Sweet Potato Fries

Serves: 4

Here is a lovely alternative to the classic french fry. And who doesn't love fries? Really. There are many root vegetable you can use in place of potatoes, so play with this recipe. Behold—your new favorite fry!

**2 lb. sweet
potatoes
(about 3-4)
3 Tbsp. grapeseed or
safflower oil
A few pinches of
sea salt**

1. Preheat the oven to 425° F. and oil two baking sheets with coconut or sunflower seed oil.
2. Slice the sweet potatoes into 1/4 inch strips (think french fries). In a large bowl toss the sweet potatoes with oil and salt.
3. Line the fries in a single layer on your two oiled baking sheet. Do not overcrowd, as the fries will just steam and be soggy.
4. Bake until golden brown, about 15–20 minutes, turning once or twice.
5. Remove from oven, let cool, and enjoy. Try not to eat them all off the pan!

Try with: Garlic Aioli, Lemon Aioli, Almond Peanut Sauce, Garden Ranch Sauce, or Cashew Sour Cream.

Creamy Mashed Parsnips

Creamy Mashed Parsnips

Serves: 4

These mashed parsnips will likely become a favorite in your household for everyday meals as well as holiday celebrations. Surprise yourself and use parsnips, a highly underrated root vegetable, in place of potatoes in this healthy, indulgent side dish.

2 lb. parsnips
2 Tbsp. extra virgin olive oil
3 Tbsp. coconut oil
¾ cup coconut milk
¾ tsp. sea salt
plus more if needed

1. Peel the parsnips and cut them into medium chunks. They don't have to be uniform, as you will be boiling and mashing them. Put them in a large (4 quart) pot, and fill with cold water, covering the parsnips by 2 inches.

2. Bring the vegetables to a boil over medium-high heat. Continue to boil until they are easily pierced with a fork, about 20 minutes. Drain and set aside.

3. In a large bowl or food processor, combine the parsnips with olive and coconut oil, coconut milk, and sea salt. Mash until creamy, adding more coconut milk as needed to yield a creamy consistency.

4. Do-ahead option for holidays: Keep the mashed parsnips warm by holding them in a covered metal bowl set over a pan of simmering water for up to an hour.

Use as a neutral side dish when serving a main dish (meat or vegetarian) that features a flavorful sauce, such as the Lemon Picatta Sauce, Charmoula, or a pesto.

Grilled Radicchio

Serves: 4

A lovely summer side dish on its own, or as part of a salad or grilled veggie plate. Cook on a grill pan inside if you don't have access to a grill.

2 heads radicchio
3 Tbsp. olive oil
½ tsp. sea salt
½ tsp. fresh ground pepper

1. Heat a grill (or a grill pan) over medium-low heat. Using a grill brush, lightly oil the grill to prevent sticking.

2. Cut the radicchio in half and remove the small stem and core by cutting a small triangle shape at the bottom (like you would with cabbage).
Cut the halves lengthwise so you have four wedges per head (8 total).

3. Brush the remaining oil onto the radicchio and sprinkle with salt and pepper.

4. Grill the radicchio, about 3–4 minutes per side, or until lightly browned and crispy.

The bitterness of radicchio is a nice offset to sweeter sauces such as the Simple Cider Sauce, Lavender Berry Chutney, or Spicy Plum Chutney, as well as richer sauces such as the Garden Ranch Sauce.

Grilled Raddichio

Quick Roasted Beets

Serves: 4

This is a two-part method to cooking beets that yields a tender, flavorful result. Rather than roast the beets for close to an hour (and get shriveled veggies), here you will parcook and then quick roast the beets (see glossary). This is a life-altering technique that I hope you will use again and again in the kitchen.

2 lb. beets (about 4 medium-size beets)
3 Tbsp. grapeseed or avocado oil
½ tsp. sea salt

1. Preheat the oven to 400° F.

2. Chop beets into bite-size pieces. I typically chop them in half (cut side down on the board for a stable surface) and cut each half into 9 pieces—three slices vertically and three horizontally.

3. Place chopped beets in a pot and cover with water, about 1–2 inches over the veggies. Add a pinch of salt to the water, turn on high heat, and cover until the water starts to boil. Boil for 4–5 minutes, then strain.

4. You now have parcooked beets! Toss the beets in a bowl with oil and salt. Spread out on a baking sheet. I like to line my baking sheets with parchment paper or a silpat (reusable silicon pan liner) so it's easier to clean.

5. Roast for 20 minutes, or until golden brown and cooked through. Toss once during cook time to brown both sides.

Variations: Use this method with any root vegetable you have on hand: carrots, rutabaga, turnips, sweet potato, celery root—you name it! Try adding in a tablespoon or two of fresh herbs as you roast, such as rosemary or thyme.

Try with: Horseradish Cream Sauce on the side, or toss with Simper Cider Sauce, or Fennel Yogurt Sauce.

Sautéed Leafies with Caramelized Onions

Serves: 4

Cooking leafy greens in olive oil yields a pretty basic and uneventful, albeit healthy, side dish. Here, fancy up your greens with sweet caramelized onions. The first step of this recipe, caramelizing onions, is a great one to have for many uses, including pizza!

¼ cup coconut oil

2 Tbsp. olive oil

2 yellow onions, sliced

½ tsp. sea salt

2 bunches kale or leafy greens of choice, destemmed and chopped

1. In a large sauté pan, heat the oils over medium-high heat.
2. Add the sliced onion and the salt. Brown the onions on medium-high heat for 5–7 minutes, stirring occasionally.
3. Once most of the onions are brown on one side, reduce the heat to low and caramelize the onions for 20–30 minutes more, stirring occasionally.
4. Add your kale or leafy green of choice and 1/3 cup water. Bring heat to high and cover the skillet to steam the kale, about 3 minutes only.
5. Season with a few pinches of salt and pepper, stir to combine the kale and onions, and taste.

Try with: Any of the pestos stirred into the pan at the end of cooking. Lovely with Romesco Sauce, Garden Ranch Sauce, or with a dollop of Lemon Aioli.

PART 2

The Magical World of Sauces

IMAGINE A GOOD WITCH OVER A BOILING CAULDRON, tossing and sprinkling in unique ingredients to make a magical potion that will heal someone or make someone incredibly happy. This is precisely what sauce making is like to me. The next five chapters of this book are devoted to the tantalizing art of making glorious, nutritious sauces. Please be prepared to grab your proverbial wand and get chopping, blending, and brewing some divine concoctions.

People often ask my family if I've always been interested in cooking. The answer they give is "yes," and the story they usually share involves the early phases of my sauce making as a preteen. My mother amazingly prepared dinner for our family of five nearly every night I can remember, and we all sat down as a family to eat. She would typically make a green salad with the main course. At some point I started offering to whip up a salad dressing for her. I would grab ingredients and tinker, without being aware that I was striving for perfect balance— Dijon mustard, red wine vinegar, olive oil, maple syrup. Sometimes raspberry jam. Sometimes olive juice. These ingredients separately sound unrelated in sequence. However, blended or shaken into a sauce they become something new. Something interesting and cravable. Something beyond the ingredients themselves.

Some 20 years later, I still approach sauce making the same way. I grab this and that, moving quickly and instinctively, constantly focused on the balance of flavor as well as texture. Sauces can enhance foods beautifully and don't have to be heavy and full of ingredients you should generally avoid. Rather, you can focus on ingredients that are designed with freshness (like herbs), brightness (like citrus and vinegar), and robustness (like olive oil or miso) in mind.

Each of the sauce recipes that follow in Chapters 5–9 are ones I've made for years. In fact, several are the original recipes I used for my sauce line sold in grocery stores in the Northwest between 2009–2012.

If you were a fan of these sauces, such as the Nude Ranch, Turmeric Coconut, Dream Date Sauce, or Nude Pudding, you are in luck! You can now make these at home, and cherish the recipes forever. I love sharing the good things in life.

CHAPTER 3
Savory Sauces

SAVORY IS A BLANKET TERM USED TO DESCRIBE A complex flavor field. It is often defined by what it is not: it is not overly sweet, nor spicy, nor straight-up salty or sour. It is a balanced combination of several of these flavors that develops into a new (savory) flavor experience.

Several of these sauces are sharp, bright, and at the same time well spiced and versatile. These are thinner sauces that can be drizzled over your fish or chicken (Lemon Picatta or Romesco), tossed into a grain dish such as rice or pasta (Turmeric Coconut or Raw Tomato), or tossed into a salad (Charmoula). Don't be limited to these suggested uses alone, however. These are some of the most versatile sauces in this book. Enjoy!

Charmoula

Charmoula

Makes: 2 cups

This sauce wakes up anything you pair with it. Be it vegetables, fish, meat, or grain, you are in for a brightly flavored treat when you make this sauce. It's one of the most versatile and is definitely a crowd pleaser.

2 tsp. ground cumin
2 garlic cloves
2 cups cilantro, chopped
(1 large bunch)
2 cups parsley, chopped
(1 large bunch)
½ cup lemon juice
¼ tsp. cayenne pepper
¾ cup olive oil
½ tsp. salt, to taste
¼–⅓ cup water to thin,
as needed

Combine ingredients in a blender and blend until smooth. Season to taste.

Try with: Grilled meats, vegetable fritters, salads, grain dishes, sautéed vegetables, and any other thing you fancy dipping or drizzling with this bold and beautiful sauce.

Raw Tomato Sauce

Makes: 3 cups

During summer and autumn, this is a fantastic recipe which requires zero cooking and thus, no standing and sweating over a hot stove. If you want some added texture, add a small handful of pine nuts toward the end of blending.

½ cup sun-dried tomatoes, soaked
3–4 large tomatoes
¼ cup fresh basil
1 clove garlic
4–5 dates, pitted
1 carrot, chopped
½ tsp. sea salt
2–3 Tbsp. olive oil
water to thin (optional)

1. Soak the sun-dried tomatoes in warm water for 15–20 minutes.
2. In a food processor blend together the tomatoes, sun-dried tomatoes, basil, and garlic until well blended.
3. Add the dates, carrot, salt, and olive oil and blend until smooth. This sauce should be thick, but you can certainly add water to thin it out!

Try with: Grilled summer vegetables, zucchini noodles, grilled chicken, or pasta.

Raw Tomato Sauce

Lemon Picatta Sauce

Makes: 1 cup (4 servings)

This sauce comes together in part by panfrying lightly breaded fish or chicken (or vegetables), so plan on seasoning whatever you are cooking. For a simple picatta-style fish or chicken I love using almond flour, nutritional yeast, salt, and dried oregano as a well-seasoned breading, mixing ingredients to taste. This breading will impart a great flavor and will also function to thicken the sauce.

¼ cup white wine
½ cup freshly squeezed lemon juice (2 lemons)
2 Tbsp. olive oil
2 Tbsp. coconut oil
¾ tsp. salt
½ tsp. freshly ground black pepper
3 Tbsp. capers in brine, drained
½ cup fresh parsley, chopped

1. After you are finished browning your fish or chicken or veggies in a pan (using equal parts coconut and olive oil for panfrying), you are ready to start this quick pan sauce.

2. Over medium heat, add the wine and lemon juice to the pan. Scrape the pan with a wooden spoon to incorporate all the brown bits from panfrying. Add the olive and coconut oil, salt, and pepper, continuing to scrape the pan. The sauce should be bubbling; if it's not, turn up the heat until it is, as you are looking to reduce the sauce.

3. Add the capers and cook until the sauce is slightly thick, about 2 minutes. Add in the parsley and pour the sauce over your prepared fish, chicken, or veggies.

Try with: Wild sole or pounded chicken breasts for an easy meal. Pair with a salad and you are done. For a vegetarian entrée, try breading the Herb and Chickpea Croquettes instead of an animal protein.

Romesco Sauce

Makes: 2 cups

This is my take on a classic Spanish sauce. Traditionally, romesco contains bread crumbs from stale bread and has a nice texture to it. My version is grain-free and gives you an option to make a very smooth or semi-textured sauce, depending on what you like.

12 whole almonds, toasted
2 red peppers, roasted,*
peeled, and seeded
½ cup cherry tomatoes,**
roasted
2 Tbsp. ground flaxseed
2–3 Tbsp. red wine vinegar
or sherry vinegar
2 cloves garlic
one pinch–¼ tsp. cayenne
pepper
¾ tsp. salt
⅓ cup olive oil
½ cup almond flour

1. Pulse almonds in a food processor or blender until ground.
2. Add roasted pepper, tomatoes, flaxseed, vinegar, garlic, cayenne pepper, and salt to the almonds and process until smooth, drizzling in olive oil slowly to incorporate consistently. Add almond flour to thicken the sauce slightly, pulsing until just incorporated. Season with 1 more tablespoon vinegar to taste, if desired.

*To roast the peppers: place rinsed peppers over a direct flame if you have a gas burner, rotating the peppers using tongs to char all sides. Once all sides of the peppers are blackened, place them in a metal bowl and cover tightly with plastic wrap or parchment paper and a rubber band. Allow peppers to steam for 10 minutes, then peel them by running under cold water. Blackened skin and seeds will wash away and you will have nicely roasted peppers. If you don't have an open flame burner, cover peppers in foil with a drizzle of oil and roast at 450° F. until blackened, about 25–30 minutes. Follow steps to steam and peel.

**To roast the tomatoes: in a medium oven-safe skillet or baking dish, toss tomatoes with a drizzle of oil and a pinch of salt. Roast at 450° F. until tomatoes swell and blister slightly, about 15 minutes.

Try with: Roasted root vegetables or potatoes, Quinoa Sweet Potato Cakes, Herb and Chickpea Croquettes, or on fish or chicken.

Tangy Parsley Sauce

Makes: 1 cup

Umeboshi plum paste can be found in the international section of your grocery store, or at Asian markets (see glossary). A little goes a long way. No added salt is needed when you use this amazing sauce in recipes!

1 large bunch parsley
1 bunch scallions
⅓ cup extra-virgin olive oil
3 Tbsp. umeboshi plum paste (or 3 Tbsp. + 1 tsp. umeboshi plum vinegar)
1 heaping Tbsp. chickpea miso, to taste
¾ cup water

1. Coarsely chop parsley and scallions and add to blender.
2. Add remaining ingredients and process until smooth.

Try with: Rice or bean dishes, salads, as a dipping sauce for salad wraps, on sautéed vegetables, or drizzled over white fish for a distinctive, tangy flavor.

Turmeric Coconut Curry Sauce

Makes: 3 cups

This is a neutral, subtle sauce that is quite popular and very versatile for everyday cooking. Look for the thick coconut milk (see glossary) that often settles at the top of the can. To encourage the thickness, chill your cans of coconut milk when you bring them home from the store.

2 cups thick coconut milk
1 Tbsp. ground turmeric
2 tsp. curry powder
1 tsp. garam masala
½ tsp. ground cumin and/ or ¼ tsp. cayenne pepper (optional add-ins!)
¼ cup lime juice
¾ tsp. sea salt

1. Bring coconut milk and spices to a simmer.
2. Stir in lime juice and salt to taste. Sauce thickens slightly when chilled.

Try with: Chicken, fish, whole grains, cooked vegetables, or as a dipping sauce for the Daikon Scallion Fritters.

Turmeric Coconut Curry Sauce

CHAPTER 4
Creamy Sauces

CREAMY IS THE DREAMIEST TEXTURE. Especially alongside crunchy, crispy foods. It's a consistency we crave in our diets from a young age, and one that doesn't have to come in the form of ice cream or other dairy products exclusively.

Over the past decade I've devoted time and energy to creating delicious, indulgent seeming, creamy sauces and condiments that are suitable for people who choose or have to eliminate dairy from their diets. I also do this without using any soy products such as tofu, to appeal to the crowd who passes on soy due to health or environmental reasons.

So, after much tweaking and perfecting, I share with you some of my favorite creamy sauces and dips for you to enjoy, no matter how you love to eat. Play with variations on these recipes and you'll have double the fun. Chop in fresh herbs, add more spice, or whatever suits your fancy. Since creamy sauces tend to be thicker, it's helpful to have a good blender for these recipes. Enjoy!

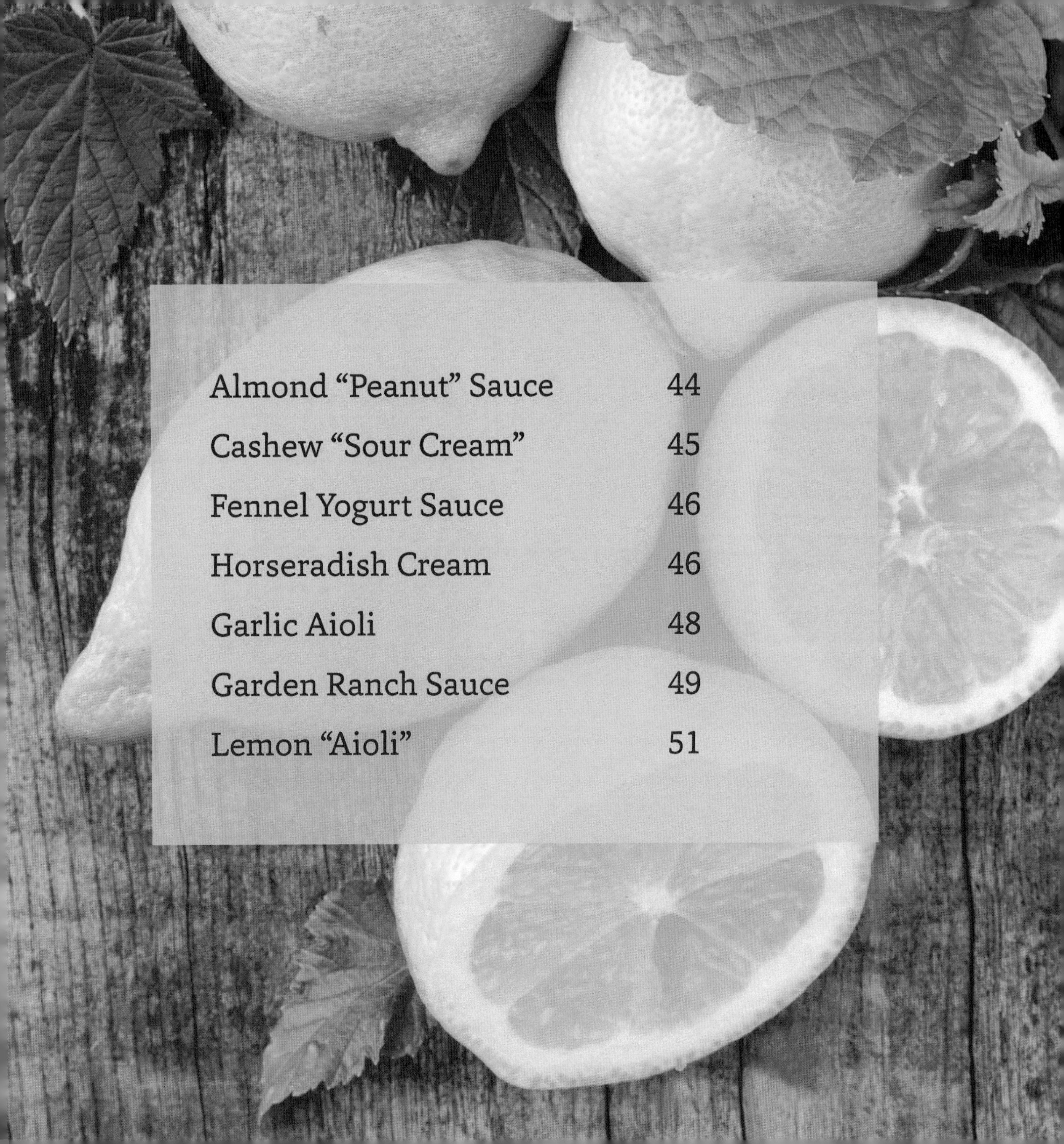

Almond "Peanut" Sauce

Makes: 1 ½ cups

Don't be mistaken, my version of a "peanut sauce" contains no peanuts. It also contains no soy of any kind, making it a great choice for most all kinds of eaters. If you or a loved one can't have nuts, try substituting sunflower butter in place of the almond butter.

½ cup almond butter
2–3 Tbsp. ginger, chopped
⅓ cup coconut milk or coconut water
3–4 Tbsp. lemon juice
2 Tbsp. raw honey or maple syrup
½ Tbsp. sesame oil or olive oil
¼ tsp. cayenne pepper
1 clove garlic (optional)
¼ jalepeno pepper, seeded and chopped (optional)
1 pinch sea salt

Use a blender to blend all ingredients, adding a pinch of salt, to taste.

Try with: Spring rolls, salad wraps, chicken satay, and raw carrots —it's a great dipping sauce!

Cashew "Sour Cream"

Makes: 2 cups

This dairy-free, nut-based cream is a common recipe in my kitchen. If you have nut allergies you can use pine nuts since they are actually a seed and not a nut! A high-speed blender makes this sauce very smooth and velvety, so plan to add more water and olive oil if you are working with a typical blender. It will be delicious either way.

2 cups raw cashew pieces, soaked (or 1⅔ cups cashew butter)
1 tsp. sea salt
2 Tbsp. apple cider vinegar
3 Tbsp. lemon juice
¼ cup olive oil
¼ cup water, or more to thin

1. Cover cashew pieces with room-temperature water and soak, 4 hours or more.
2. Drain and rinse cashews. Place in a high-speed blender with all ingredients.
3. Purée until completely smooth, about 2–3 minutes. Thin with more water (or a bit of olive oil) if there is still a gritty texture to the sauce due to a low-powered blender.
4. Add various ingredients for variations on the theme: stir in chopped herbs, chives, or marinated artichokes.

Try with: Any of the fritter recipes, roasted vegetables, broiled asparagus, grilled vegetables, and any crudités. Also great as a garnish for soup.

Fennel Yogurt Sauce

Makes: 1 1/2 cups

Here is a nice, refreshing sauce that isn't too thick. You can serve it with Mediterranean dishes and turn up the heat by adding more cayenne and cumin for a kick! Chopped mint is also a nice addition if you are looking to stay on the cooler side.

½ **head fennel, chopped (about ¾ cup)**
1 cup coconut milk (or goat milk yogurt, if tolerated)
2 Tbsp. lemon juice, to taste
½ tsp. sea salt
⅛–¼ tsp. cayenne pepper
½ tsp. cumin, ground

Blend all ingredients in a food processor for a textured sauce, or run in a blender for an entirely smooth sauce. Adjust seasonings as desired.

Try with: Cucumbers, as a salad dressing, on lamb or beef skewers, gyro sandwiches, or falafel.

Horseradish Cream

Makes: 1 cup

Fancy homemade horseradish? Here's a delicious, naturally spicy horseradish that doesn't contain any preservatives or dairy. This is a personal favorite. Enjoy!

1 cup thick coconut milk
¼ cup fresh horseradish, peeled and chopped
1 Tbsp. apple cider vinegar
½ tsp. sea salt, more to taste

Combine ingredients in a blender until smooth.

Try with: Roasted or grilled meats, roasted beets or beet soup, on Crispy Root Vegetable Fritters, or as a dip for crudité vegetables.

Horseradish Cream

Garlic Aioli

Makes: 2 cups

If you've ever wanted to make your own homemade aioli, here's your chance! Please note that you need to use a hand mixer or standing mixer to really make this successfully. The most important thing is to very, very slowly add in your olive oil at the beginning. Once the emulsification begins, you can add oil in a thin, steady stream, being careful not to add too much. One foolproof way to make this recipe without much fuss is to add in the yolk of a hard-boiled egg with the garlic and salt, then follow the recipe.

2–3 garlic cloves, minced
½ tsp. sea salt
4 egg yolks
1 ½–2 cups olive oil
2 tsp. fresh lemon juice

1. Let all your ingredients come to room temperature before you begin.
2. Mash garlic and salt together until they form a paste.
3. Add egg yolks and whisk vigorously with a hand mixer, a blender, or a standing mixer.
4. With the blender going full speed, slowly add olive oil, starting one drop at a time, until an emulsion begins. As you add drop-by-drop of oil, you will start to see the oil and yolk come together and the mixture will lighten in color.
5. Once the emulsion starts, you can add in the oil in a thin stream. When the aioli thickens, add lemon juice, then continue adding remaining oil. Add more lemon juice in at the end, if you desire a tangy aioli or thinner end product.

Keeps in the fridge for 3–4 days.

Try with: Roasted vegetables, on a sandwich, on fritters, or tossed with potato or egg salad.

Garden Ranch Sauce

Makes: 2 ½ cups

This is a version of the "Nude Ranch" dressing that I used to sell in grocery stores in the Northwest. It is a popular dip and dressing, even for those who don't like a standard ranch (since it's not much like your typical ranch dressing). See notes below if you don't have a high-speed blender on how to still make this yummy sauce!

1 ⅔ cups raw cashew pieces, soaked (or cashew butter*)
⅔ cup water
⅓ cup apple cider vinegar
⅓ cup olive oil
1 Tbsp. dried oregano
2 Tbsp. onion powder/ chopped onion
1 tsp. sea salt
⅓ cup fresh dill or oregano, chopped
6 scallions, thinly sliced

1. Soak your raw cashews by covering with water and let sit at room temperature for 4 hours or more, up to overnight.

2. Set the sliced scallions aside in a small bowl. Place remaining ingredients in a high-speed blender and blend until very smooth and creamy, about 1–2 minutes on high. Add up to ¼ cup more water if needed to make a creamy sauce.

3. Add in the scallions and pulse just 10–15 seconds. Keep chilled until ready to serve.

*If you don't have a high-speed blender: Try this recipe using 1 1/2 cups cashew butter. Mix in a food processor/blender, or warm the cashew butter lightly to soften and mix vigorously in a bowl until all ingredients combine and are smooth. Chill.

Try with: Grilled or roasted chicken, sweet potato fries, on a sandwich or with raw vegetables.

Lemon "Aioli"

Lemon "Aioli"

Makes: 2 cups

Here's a vegan version of aioli that is soy-free and also egg-free. If you don't have a high-speed blender, you may want to use 1 2/3 cups cashew butter in place of the cashew pieces, so that you can yield a smooth sauce no matter what machine you use.

2 cups cashews, soaked in water 4 hours or more
¼ cup lemon zest
3–4 Tbsp. lemon juice
1 clove garlic
⅓ cup water (or more to thin)
2 tsp. apple cider vinegar
¾ tsp. salt, plus more to taste

Combine ingredients in a blender and process until very smooth. Season to taste. Add more water if a thinner consistency is desired.

Variations: Add only 3 tablespoons water for a cheese-like consistency; add more water for a thinner sauce; add fresh herbs to make it a dip for crudités.

Try with: Crispy Root Vegetable Fritters, Balsamic Asparagus, Quick Roasted Beets, crab cakes, or on a sandwich.

CHAPTER 5
Pestos

PESTO, PESTO, HOW I LOVE YOU SO! In my kitchen pesto is not a sauce reserved for the summer season when basil is bountiful. Instead, pesto wears many hats throughout the seasons, playing the same, powerful role of an herb-based condiment. You can honestly use many types of nuts or seeds to make pesto (remember, pine nuts are a seed). The following pesto recipes make a thick, strongly flavored pesto that you can use to dollop on fritters and vegetables, or thin out with water and use as a sauce for pasta, meats, fish, or legumes. Be sure to start each recipe by processing the nuts or seeds with garlic and salt, so that your pesto has an even texture. As a variation, toast your nuts and seeds to add a pronounced nutty flavor. Finally, here is your chance to become familiar with one of my favorite ingredients, chickpea miso, which is a fermented bean paste made from chickpeas rather than soy (see glossary). If you can't find it and can tolerate soy in your diet, look for a basic white miso in the refrigerated section of your grocery store. A little goes a long way to add a robust flavor!

Mint Pesto	55
Dill Pistachio Pesto	55
Rosemary Hazelnut Pesto	56
Oregano Walnut Pesto	58
Lemon Basil Pesto	59

Mint Pesto

Mint Pesto

Makes: 1 cup

This is a wonderfully refreshing take on pesto. It's a great way to use up mint if you have it growing in your garden, since it's one of the most prolific plants in summertime. Try arugula in place of spinach for a subtly spicy pesto.

½ cup almonds
½ clove garlic
¼ tsp. sea salt
2 cups mint, large stems removed
½ cup spinach, packed
1–2 Tbsp. chickpea miso
3 Tbsp. lemon juice
¼–⅓ cup olive oil

1. Put almonds, garlic, and salt in the food processer and pulse until finely ground. Add the remaining ingredients and process until smooth.
2. Thin with water if a thinner sauce is desired (up to 1 cup).

Try with: Light fish dishes, tossed with grain salads, or grilled meats or veggies. You can thin this sauce with almond milk in a pan to make a pasta sauce with gluten-free pasta. Be sure to add more salt as needed to make this sauce bold enough for noodles.

Dill Pistachio Pesto

Makes: 1 1/2 cups

This wonderful pesto can make its way into all three meals of the day. It pairs nicely with a frittata or omelet for breakfast or brunch, with poached or grilled salmon over salad for lunch, and tossed with roasted new potatoes or thinned out as a sauce over lamb for dinner. Look for large bunches of dill at your grocery or farmer's market to avoid overspending on small boxes of herbs.

2 cloves of garlic
½ cup pistachios
½ tsp. sea salt
½ cup dill, large stems removed
1 bunch parsley, large stems removed (about 1 ½ cups)
⅓ cup miso
3 Tbsp. lemon juice
¼ –⅓ cup olive oil

1. Set oil aside.
2. Put garlic, pistachios, and salt in the food processer and pulse until finely ground.
3. Add the dill and parsley and pulse until ground.
4. Add the miso, lemon juice and olive oil, and blend until smooth.
5. Thin with water if a thinner sauce is desired (up to 1 cup).

Rosemary Hazelnut Pesto

Makes: 2 cups

This is an excellent pesto for winter and more hearty side dishes or main courses. Kale is a fun substitute for the traditional parsley. Come summer, substitute basil or cilantro for the rosemary (about ½ cup) to keep this recipe current with the season.

1 clove garlic
1 cup hazelnuts, toasted
½ tsp. sea salt
½ bunch kale, destemmed
2 big sprigs rosemary
(about ¼ cup destemmed)
⅓ cup chickpea or white
miso
2 Tbsp. balsamic vinegar
or lemon juice
¾ cup olive oil

1. Combine the garlic, hazelnuts, and salt in a food processor, pulsing until evenly ground.

2. Add in the kale, rosemary, miso, and vinegar or lemon juice and keep the machine running.

3. Slowly pour in the olive oil to emulsify the ingredients. Adjust flavor and consistency as desired.

Toss with quick roasted sweet potatoes or celery root, serve with the Herb and Chickpea Croquettes, Quinoa Sweet Potato Cakes, or as a condiment with simple sautéed vegetables. Great stirred into vegetable soups for added flavor and depth, or with roasted chicken.

Rosemary Hazelnut Pesto

Oregano Walnut Pesto

Makes: 2 cups

Most of my pesto recipes originate from utilizing ingredients I am growing in my garden or have readily on hand. I encourage you to do the same, and to rotate in different ingredients as you have access to them!

1 clove garlic
1 cup walnuts, toasted
½ tsp. sea salt
½ bunch swiss chard, de-stemmed
¼ cup oregano leaves, de-stemmed and packed
⅓ cup chickpea miso
1–2 Tbsp. balsamic vinegar or lemon juice
1 cup olive oil

1. Combine the garlic, walnuts, and salt in a food processor, pulsing until evenly ground.

2. Add in the swiss chard, oregano, miso, and vinegar or lemon juice and keep the machine running.

3. Slowly pour in the olive oil to emulsify the ingredients. Adjust flavor and consistency as desired.

Try with: Roasted chicken, in white bean salads, on roasted or grilled veggies, or stirred into a soup for added flavor and depth.

Lemon Basil Pesto

Makes: 2 cups

A lovely summery pesto. Substitute pine nuts for pumpkin seeds and spinach for the parsley as a variation. Omit or reduce the lemon juice if you desire a classic pesto. Nutritional yeast, found in the bulk section of most grocery and natural foods stores, replaces the parmesan cheese traditionally found in pesto recipes.

4 cloves garlic
½ cup pumpkin seeds or
pine nuts
½ tsp. sea salt
1 ½ cup packed basil, big
stems removed
½ cup parsley
¼ cup nutritional yeast
⅓ cup lemon juice
½ cup olive oil
½ cup water, or more to
thin (if desired)

1. Combine the garlic, pumpkin seeds or pine nuts, and salt in a food processor, pulsing until evenly ground.

2. Add in the basil, parsley, nutritional yeast and lemon juice and keep the machine running.

3. Slowly pour in the olive oil to emulsify the ingredients. Adjust flavor and consistency as desired with water.

Try with: Grilled chicken, Quinoa Sweet Potato Cakes, roasted summer vegetables, or stirred into quinoa.

CHAPTER 6
Savory Fruit Sauces

FRUIT IS A FOOD GROUP THAT VERY CLEARLY SHIFTS WITH the seasons—you'll eat the best, most affordable apples in the fall and the most delicious, perfect berries in the summertime. Use nature's cues to choose your fruit in season, and you'll have wonderful results with the following sauces.

I've selected one fruit-based sauce per season: Lavender Berry Chutney for spring, Spicy Plum Chutney for summer, Simple Cider Sauce for fall, and Tamarind Glaze for winter. Tamarind is a tropical fruit and thus makes for a nice departure from the typical citrus options available during wintertime. Use fruit sauces as a counterpart to spicy and savory foods, as well as a way to offer brightness to an otherwise bland main course or side dish.

Lavender Berry Chutney	62
Spicy Plum Chutney	64
Simple Cider Sauce	65
Tamarind Glaze	65

Lavender Berry Chutney

Serves: 4

This is a perfect spring chutney when at long last berry season arrives. It's great as a condiment for main dishes and appetizers for spring brunches, lunches, and dinners.

2 pints strawberries, black-berries or raspberries
1 medium onion, minced
zest of 1 lemon
2 Tbsp. lemon juice (from 1 lemon)
1 Tbsp. garlic, minced (about 2 cloves)
¼ tsp. chili flakes
⅓ cup red wine vinegar
¾ tsp. sea salt
3 Tbsp. raw honey or coconut sugar (optional)*
2 Tbsp. fresh lavender (or 1 tsp. dried lavender)
2 Tbsp. fresh basil or mint, finely chopped

1. Combine all prepared ingredients apart from the lavender and herbs in a saucepan. Bring to a boil.
2. Continue cooking at a low, rolling boil for 15 minutes, stirring occasionally.
3. Mix in lavender and fresh herbs at the end.
*For a less-sweet chutney, omit the raw honey or coconut sugar altogether.

Try with: Grilled pork tenderloin, salmon, or any light fish recipe that has a little spice. Also nice on toast with smoked salmon.

Lavender Berry Chutney

Spicy Plum Chutney

Serves 4–6

This is a Southern Indian–inspired recipe that offers a nice balance of spicy, sweet, and savory flavors. I offer a few optional add-ins depending on what you like. I love this with fresh ginger, cilantro, and scallions all together!

4 plums, pits removed and coarsely chopped
¾ tsp. chili flakes
⅓ cup olive oil
2 Tbsp. honey or coconut sugar
¼ tsp. salt

Optional add-ins:
½ bunch cilantro
4 scallions, chopped
2 cloves garlic or 2 inches of ginger

1. Blend all ingredients until smooth (or leave some texture by prepping in a food processor).
2. Heat until simmering on the stove, just 3–4 minutes. Done!

Try with: Spicy indian foods such as dahl, pakoras, and curry seasoned fish. Also nice on grilled meats in the summertime.

Simple Cider Sauce

Serves: 4

This recipe is for braising leafy greens, in particular. Start with blanched (see glossary) greens, or simply sauté them in a little olive oil, then add in this reduced sauce. The tart sweetness of apple cider provides a nice balance to bitter greens of all kinds.

¾ cup apple cider
1 Tbsp. olive oil or coconut oil
2 garlic cloves, minced
1 Tbsp. apple cider vinegar
¾ tsp. sea salt
½ tsp. red pepper flakes

1. Heat apple cider and reduce at a rapid boil for 4–5 minutes, or until reduced by half.
2. Add in the remaining ingredients and lower heat, cooking for 3–4 minutes more or until sauce thickens enough to coat the back of a spoon.
3. Stir in cooked greens until coated, seasoning with salt and pepper to taste.

Try with: Leafy greens, or roasted or braised pork.

Tamarind Glaze

Serves 4–6

This is a great glaze for fish or meat as well as stir-fried vegetables. You will know the glaze is ready when the sauce coats the back of a spoon nicely without the oil separating. If you are storing extra for later, keep in a glass jar and be sure to stir it well before reheating. Tamarind paste can be found in the Asian section of your grocery store.

2–3 Tbsp. tamarind paste
⅓ cup orange juice
¼ cup molasses
¼ cup coconut sugar
¼ tsp. crushed red pepper flakes
2 Tbsp. ginger, minced
2 Tbsp. lime juice

Combine all ingredients together in a pot and bring to a rolling boil, stirring occasionally. Reduce sauce by one-third the volume, until it coats the back of a spoon nicely.

Try with: Chicken skewers, roasted fish, or toss with stir-fried vegetables.

CHAPTER 7
Dessert Sauces

EVERYTHING IS BETTER WITH A SWEET ENDING. There are four sauces that, while versatile only in Dessert Land, are recipes that I couldn't leave out of this book. Two of these dessert sauces are original recipes that eventually became available commercially in the Northwest when I had my Abby's Table line of sauces in grocery stores and at farmer's markets around Portland.

Each sauce is free of dairy and refined sugar, making it a delightful way to end a meal or enjoy a treat on its own. I use healthy fats such as coconut and avocado to balance the blood sugar spike that comes with most desserts, so you can have your pudding and eat it, too!

Almost Nude Pudding

Makes: 4 cups

For all the Nude Pudding fanatics out there, I am pleased to share my original recipe for the divine chocolate sauce that I sold in grocery stores in the Northwest years ago. One of the secret ingredients, ground star anise, is available in the bulk spice section of grocery stores or occasionally in jars. If you are brave enough to open young coconuts, you are in for a treat, though a banana works just as well.

2 small ripe avocadoes, pitted
1 banana or meat of 1 young coconut
½ cup coconut butter, cut into chunks
¾ cup cocoa or carob powder
½ cup raw honey
½ cup maple syrup
1 tsp. ground star anise
2 tsp. ground cinnamon
1 tsp. vanilla extract
1 cup coconut milk or coconut water
¼ tsp. sea salt

1. Blend all ingredients in a high-speed blender.
2. Swoon. Be full of love and this pudding.

Keeps in the fridge for 4–5 days, if it lasts that long.

Try with: Fresh fruit, in a fruit parfait, as a layer to a cake and berry parfait, or just eat in a bowl on its own.

Almost Nude Pudding

Amaretto Coconut Caramel Sauce

Makes: 1 cup

Coconut appears in many forms in this recipe. For a low-glycemic caramel option, try coconut nectar, which is available in the sweetener section of most organic grocery stores. Chill overnight for a true caramel consistency, or serve warm for a thinner dessert sauce.

1 cup coconut sugar
1 cup coconut cream (or thick coconut milk)
¼ cup maple syrup or coconut nectar
2 Tbsp. coconut oil
2 Tbsp. amaretto

1. In medium saucepan, combine all ingredients except the amaretto.
2. Bring to a boil, whisking occasionally.
3. Reduce heat, boil gently on medium high, about 10–11 minutes, or until slightly thickened (mixture should coat the back of a spoon nicely).
4. Remove from the heat. Stir in amaretto.
5. Chill in the fridge overnight before using, as the sauce will be thinner when warm.

Try with: Ice cream, over cakes, or any place you'd like to use a caramel sauce.

Coconut Sweet Cream

Makes 2 ½ cups

Sometimes you really need a light whipped cream or sweet cream to top a dessert. If you are looking for a thick whipped cream consistency, then it's imperative to chill your cans of coconut milk overnight, so that the thick cream settles on the top. If you don't mind a thinner sweet cream, you can proceed with cans that are not chilled.

1 ½ cups thick coconut milk (top of two chilled cans)
stevia, to taste (powdered or drops)
2 Tbsp. tapioca flour
1 tsp. vanilla extract

1. Sweeten thick coconut milk with stevia, to taste. Add tapioca flour and whisk until blended.
2. Flavor the coconut cream with vanilla.
3. Chill until ready to serve. Freeze 30 minutes to set quickly if necessary.

Try with: Pies, cakes, cobblers, crisps, or with chocolate mousse.

Dream Date Sauce

Dream Date Sauce

Makes: 2 cups

This is another crowd favorite, the original recipe that I crafted into my line of sauces. It's a dreamy sauce that is sweetened just with dates. Enjoy!

1 cup water
½ cup cashew butter (or soaked raw cashews)
1½ cups date paste or pitted dates
2 Tbsp. vanilla extract
1 cup coconut milk
¼ tsp. sea salt
1 Tbsp. lemon juice (or more, to taste)

Blend all ingredients in a high-speed blender until very smooth and creamy, about 2–3 minutes. Sauce thickens when chilled.

Try with: Berries, yogurt and fruit, dolloped on oatmeal or pancakes, or just eaten as a pudding.

TROUBLESHOOTING
How to Balance and Correct in the Kitchen

LIFE IS FULL OF ERROR, AND NO ONE IS PERFECT. Maybe you are taking some precious time out of your busy schedule to cook, but you find yourself multitasking and maybe, just maybe, you skip a step, forget an ingredient, or walk away from the kitchen and start to burn whatever you are cooking. Or maybe you just mismeasure an ingredient and upon tasting, you realize you need a remedy for your experimental creation.

Look no further! Here is your troubleshooting guide to correct and balance flavors.

PROBLEM	SOLUTION
Too Bland	Add ½–1 teaspoon of lemon juice or vinegar, or a couple pinches of salt.
Too Salty	Add more volume, be it more vegetables, liquid, herbs, or oil to balance out the salt content. Adding a sweetener will just hide salt slightly, so go for bulking up instead.
Too Sweet	Add an acid (lemon or lime juice or vinegar) to taste, a bit more salt, or more volume if you can.
Too Sour	Add more oil or more sweetener, depending on whether your dish is savory or sweet. Adding more freshness with herbs along with the oil will help, too. Salt will make it worse.
Too Spicy	Add some fat (such as olive oil) to tone down the heat. You can add something sweet as well, if it makes sense, but an oil is your best bet.
Too Burnt	Whatever you do, don't scrape the bottom of the pan or pot! Try to gently spoon what you can off the top and work to fix that and toss the rest. Balance burnt flavors with sweeteners such as honey and add salt or a hint of lemon.
Too Thin	If you were trying to reduce a sauce, you should keep going. Wait until the sauce coats the back of a spoon. If you are blending and the sauce is too thin, add more volume in the form of ground or soaked nuts, herbs, or vegetables, whatever makes sense for the recipe.
Too Thick	Thin with water or an acid such as lemon juice or vinegar, if it won't overpower the flavor too much.
Too Chunky	Keep blending or processing!

GLOSSARY

Basic Ingredients

APPLE CIDER VINEGAR

Purchase raw apple cider vinegar, which still contains healthful enzymes that aid in digestion. Apple cider vinegar is readily available, and if it's raw, you should be able to see a culture inside the bottle—don't be alarmed!

BALSAMIC VINEGAR

There are a range of balsamic vinegars out there. I prefer organic brands that are from California or Italy. Make sure if they are aged that they contain no added sugars to thicken them.

CHICKPEA MISO

Find miso in the refrigerated section of your grocery store, often near where hummus, salsa, and guacamole are located. My favorite brand is Miso Masters. Chickpea miso has a nice, buttery and robust flavor similar to white miso (which is a good option if you can't locate chickpea miso).

COCONUT MILK

It's hard to find coconut milk these days without it containing some kind of emulsifier such as guar gum. If you are lucky enough to find a brand that is pure coconut milk, buy it! Look for organic coconut milk in BPA-free cans or in small cartons.

COCONUT OIL

Look for unrefined coconut oil when possible. Coconut oil is a great medium-high heat oil, with a heat threshold of 350° F., exactly like butter. It's a very digestible fat that has many amazing health benefits: it's anti-inflammatory and contains high amounts of healthy cholesterol to support the heart. It's by far my preferred oil when I need medium-high heat cooking and baking.

EXTRA VIRGIN OLIVE OIL

Look for cold processed olive oil from California, Italy, or Spain. Make sure it is pure olive oil and not cut with any other type of oil (labeled "blend"). Unrefined olive oil is good for no-heat, low-heat, and low–medium heat cooking only, as it has a smoke point of 325° F. You can find refined olive oils that are suitable for slightly higher heat, but I don't really use them.

GRAPESEED OIL

A decent, albeit refined, oil for high-heat cooking. Has a heat threshold of 485° F. and is a fine substitute for canola oil or other vegetable oils you might be using currently. Avocado oil is probably the best quality high-heat option, with a smoke point of 520° F. However, it is often quite pricey and thus I don't often list it in recipes.

LARD

Rendered animal fat is making a comeback. With a heat threshold of 375° F., it is an option for both panfrying and medium-high heat oven cooking. It's also very digestible to the body, and not refined like other high-heat oils. Ghee (clarified butter) is another high heat animal-based option, with a smoke point of over 450° F.

UMEBOSHI VINEGAR

Find umeboshi vinegar in the Asian section of grocery stores. A little goes a long way, so you can get away with a small bottle if you find it. This is a very alkalizing vinegar, so you can use it medicinally as well if you have a headache or a hangover! Add a teaspoon to a glass of warm water, and in a little while you should feel better.

Terms & Techniques

BLANCH

This technique is much quicker than most people realize! Bring a pot of water to a boil, and drop in your vegetable for just 1–2 minutes. For green beans and asparagus, I often just wait until they turn bright green then I quickly sweep them out of the hot water after only 30 seconds or so. Submerge in ice-cold water or if you don't have access to ice, run them constantly under cold water until no heat remains.

PANFRY

In my recipes, this is a low-oil method for crisping ingredients in a pan. Add a thin layer of medium-high to high-heat oil in a pan and add your ingredients, be it parcooked potatoes or fritters. Wait until a golden brown skin forms on the first side before flipping. Cook until nicely browned, replenishing oil as needed, and keeping the oil from smoking.

PARCOOK

This is the first of a two-step method for cooking vegetables, primarily. To parcook or parboil is to partially boil or blanch an ingredient, until nearly fork tender. You can then proceed to cooking the ingredient with some oil or fat and seasonings, so that you yield a wonderful texture and don't need to overcook the vegetable (see quick roast).

QUICK ROAST

This is the second part of cooking parcooked vegetables. Once you have blanched or parboiled your ingredients, you can finish them in the oven with oil and seasonings until lightly crisp and cooked through. Roast for 15–20 minutes or until desired consistency is reached.

ABBY FAMMARTINO has been celebrated as a healthy "dinner party diva" by Bon Appétit magazine and Portland Monthly magazine for making healthful eating entertaining and a delicious experience for all. Since graduating from the Natural Gourmet Institute of Food and Health in New York City, Abby's culinary endeavors have fed the likes of diners at Greens in San Francisco, private chef clients in Philadelphia, New York, and Seattle, supper club guests and partygoers in Portland, dinner guests in Italy, and even scientists and oceanographers on a National Geographic charter in the Aleutian Islands to hunt down a WWII submarine. Abby is able to easily craft inventive and delicious allergy-friendly cuisine that everyone loves. An avid traveler, she brings worldly twists on local and seasonal ingredients to her recipes.

abby's table

Sign up for Chef Abby's weekly inspiration newsletter for recipes, lifestyle tips, and more cooking resources at abbys-table.com.

Chef Abby's website with more recipes, weekly blog tips and events: **www.abbys-table.com**

Contact Chef Abby at **info@abbys-table.com**

For private consultations, contact Chef Abby at (503) 828-7662.

For group glasses and hands-on dinner parties, email **info@abbys-table.com**

Facebook: **Abby's Table** / Instagram: **abbycookswith**

Pinterest: **Abby's Table** / Twitter: **#abbystable**

www.abbys-table.com

Made in the USA
Lexington, KY
07 May 2016